NEWARK:
60 YEARS OF WEATHER
(1951-2010)

by

Ian Lyall

60 YEARS OF NEWARK WEATHER
(1951-2010)

by Ian Lyall

ISBN:978-1-4467-9841-7

Ian Lyall asserts the intellectual right as author of this work.

Published by Lulu.

PREFACE

I can have been no more than ten years old when a school-teacher living next door showed me how to read the temperature, and by age twelve I received a (somewhat unusual but welcome) Christmas gift of a Six's maximum-minimum thermometer.

January 1949 saw the start of daily weather records, which I have maintained in Newark-on-Trent since- with assistance during absence. I publish this work now on the records from 1951, and for the sixty years following. There are two reasons. Firstly, I do not fully trust my method of 'filling-the-gaps' for 1949-50, and also we now end at a '0' year.

I have made two moves since then, and an accompanying map shows the three sites where my records are based. Additionally, whereas my first records of temperature were with a thermometer fixed to a sheltered north-facing wall, I acquired a screen in 1971 (this was made for me by Margaret, my wife), upgrading three years later to a Stevenson Screen- with rainfall collected in a Snowdon rainguage). The move to our present address necessitated something more primitive (Six's on a shetered fencing) and then a radio-transmitter thermometer. Most recently I bought a combined temperature/pressure/humudity radio-transmitter, housed in a louvered box, made by my son-in-law Ian Bradford.

Newark-on-Trent, January 2011

THANKS

My thanks are due to the may people who along the way have helped me:

My late father (Alexander Lyall) for encouragement, and for keeping records during absences at university and during National Service.

My wife, Margaret for further encouragement, and for making my first screen.

And for constructive criticism

Messrs Vernon Ratcliffe and Charles Sutherland for making their records available to cover some holidays.

My son-in-law, Ian Bradford, for my latest upgrade screen.

Georg Müller for permission to use weather charts from the website wetterzentrale.de

Location of Observing Sites

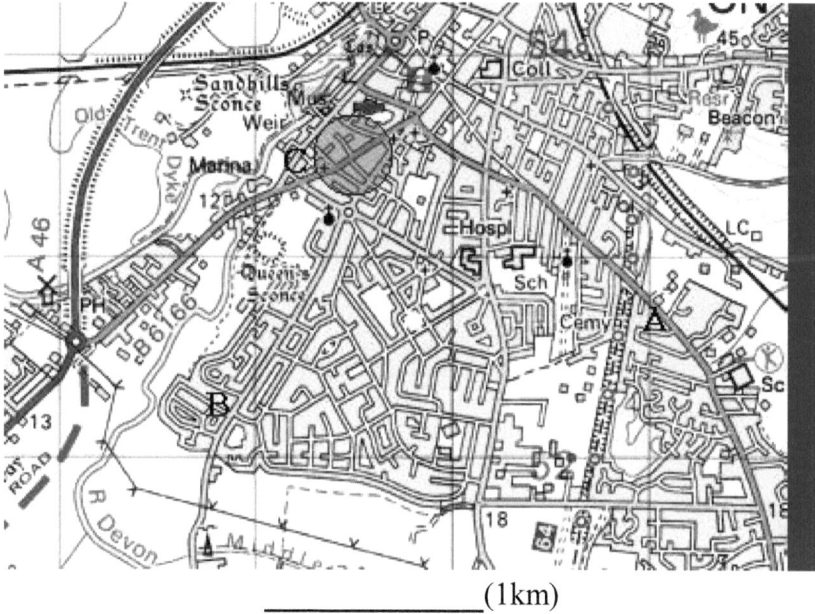

_____(1km)

A. London Road, New Balderton (up to January 1965)

B. Riverside Road, Newark-on-Trent (February 1965-May 1993

C. Coopers Yard, Newark-on-Trent (June 1993 to present)

CONTENTS

Chapter 1: The long-term data...p9

Chapter 2: Outstanding Weather events.......................p41

Chapter 3: Climate trends (short and long-term)..........p59

Appendix...p63

A. Year-by-Year...p63

B. Photographs..,,,,,,,,,,,,,,,p66

C. Useful Web-sites, reading, personal note................p72

Chapter One

The Long-term Data

The object of this chapter is to present a look at the overall weather of Newark-on-Trent for the last 60 years. Whilst the data in respect of temperature will be dominant, other elements will be taken into account, in respect of rainfall, as well as occurences of frost, snow, fog, hail and thunder.

Newark's geographical position is obviously relevant to the sort of weather we would expect. Newark is situated at 53.1° North and 50' west. It is about 15metres amsl, situated as it is in the valley of the River Trent. The climate of Britain as a whole is 'Cool, Temperate'- which means cool summers and mild winters.

Lying at a low altitude, and well to be east and south of the main high ground (the Pennines and the Welsh mountains), with lesser high levels providing further shelter (the Peak District, the Belvoir hills and the Lincoln Edge), so Newark avoids most extreme weather events.

Being on the eastern side of England, rainfall is low, and Newark enjoys relative summer warmth. Northerly winds bring most of the colder and snowier winter weather (snow of any significant depth is a rarity). Continental winds need to be east of south for any hard frosts. In winter north-easterlies can bring some snow, whilst the longer North Sea crossing means that in the summer half of the year, low clouds can spoil a fine spell.

After a brief resume of each year, we turn to look at the long-term temperature record.

1951. Avg max 13.0C, min 6.3C

Year's highest, 26.1C on 1 July/4 August, lowest -5.6C on 13 December Highest minimum 17.2C on 4 August, lowest maximum -0.6C on 29 January.

1952. Avg max 13.2C, min 6.3C

Year's highest, 28.9C on 28,30 June, lowest -7.2C on 27 January. Highest minimum 19.4C on 1 July, lowest maximum 0.0C on 27 January.

1953 Avg max 13.9C, min 7.1C

Year's highest 32.2C on 12 August, lowest -3.3C on 8 February/5 March. Highest minimum 18.9C on 13 August, lowest maximum 0.6C on 19 January.

1954. Avg max 13.3C, min 6.5C

Year's highest 27.2C on 1 September, lowest -7.8C on 4 February.Highest minimum 16.7C on 4 July, lowest maximum -1.1C on 28 January/1 February. (Highest up to 31 August only 25.5C, redeemed on 1 Sept.)

1955. Avg max 13.5C, min 6.3C

Year's highest 27.8C on 27/28 July, lowest -10.6C on 28 February. Highest minimum 18.9C on 18 July, lowest maximum -0.6C on 17 January. (A cold winter prolonged into March- avg max 6.9C, min 0.1C)

1956. Avg max 12.8C min 6.0C.

Year's highest 26.1C on 8 July, lowest -8.9C on 2 February. Highest minimum 16.1C on 9,24 July, lowest maximum -2.2C on 1,2 February (poorest summer for the 60 years)

1957. Avg max 13.9C, min 7.1C

Year's highest 30.6C on 28 June, lowest -3.3C on 20 February/8 December. Highest minimum 17.2C on 7 July, lowest maximum 1.7C on 16 December.

1958 Avg max 13.3C, min 6.8C

Year's highest 26.7C on 10 August, lowest -6.1C on 24 January. Highest minimum 16.7C on 6 September, lowest maximum -0.6C on 24 January.

1959. Avg max 15.0C, min 7.0C

Year's highest 33.3C on 5 July, lowest -5.6C on 11,16 January. Highest minimum 18.3C on 25 August, lowest maximum -1.1C on 14,16 January

Summer was one of the best, amidst many poor ones.

1960. Avg max 13.8C, 7.0C

Year's highest 31.1C on 18 June, lowest -4.4C on 14 January, Highest minimum 17.2C on 18 June, lowest minimum 1.1C on 13,14 January.

1961 Avg max 14.1C min 6.8C

Year's highest 30.0C on 30 June, lowest -6.1C on 25,29 December, Highest minimum 16.7C on 16 September, lowest maximum -1.7C on 28 December. (Very mild Feb/March: frost free, March highs up to 18C)

1962. Avg max 12.6C min 5.6C

Year's highest 26.1C on 9 June, lowest -9.4C on 3 January. Highest minimum 16.7C on 20 August, lowest maximum -1.7C on 25,29 December

1963 Avg max 12.5C, min 5.7C

Year's highest 27.8C on 12 June, lowest -11.7C on 23 January. Highest minimum 16.7C on 24 July, lowest maximum -6.1C on 24 January (Coldest winter for Britain since 1740)

1964 Avg max 13.5C, min 6.8C

Year's highest 28.3C on 26 August, lowest -6.7C on 29 December. Highest minimum 17.2C on 26 July/2 August, lowest maximum -1.7C on 16 December.

1965 Avg max 13.3C, min 5.7C

Year's highest 29.4C on 14 May, lowest -10.0C on 3 March. Highest minimum 15.6C on 13 June, lowest maximum -1.7C on 28 December (Year's maximum on 14 May)

1966. Avg max 13.4C, min 6.0C

Year's highest 27.8C on 17,19 August, lowest -7.8C on 19 January. Highest minimum 17.8C on 12 August, lowest maximum -1.1C on 19 January.

1967 Avg max 13.2C, min 5.8C

Year's highest 31.1C on 17 July, lowest -6.9C on 9 January. Highest minimum 17.0C on 17 July, lowest maximum -0.9C on 20 December

1968 Avg max 13.5C, min 5.6C

Year's highest 33.0C on 1 July, lowest -8.8C on 10 January. Highest minimum 15.0C on 1,15 July, lowest maximum -1.0C on 10 January

1969 Avg max 12.9C min 5.4C

Year's highest 33.1C on 16 July, lowest -10.4C on 8 February. Highest minimum 16.6C on 10 August, lowest maximum -1.0C on 16 February (very wintry Feb with avg max 2.3C, min -2.2C 20 frosts, 13 days with snow)

1970 Avg max 13.8C min 5.7C

Year's highest 33.2C on 7 July, lowest -9.9C on 7 January. Highest minimum 16.8C on 8 July, lowest maximum -2.6C on 7 January. Rain

597.4mm on 167 days

1971 Avg max 13.8C, min 5.7C

Year's highest 29.5C on 30 June, lowest -8.2C on 5 January. Highest minimum 16.0C on 24 July, lowest maximum -3.3C on 3 January Rain 562.3mm on 149 days. Wettest 46.1mm on 5 July.

1972. Avg max 13.2C, min 5.5C

Year's highest 27.0C on 20 July, lowest -10.2C on 31 January. Highest minimum 14.8C on 7 August, lowest maximum -2.9C on 31 January Rain 593.7mm on 168 days. Wettest 47.8mm on 9 September

1973 Avg max 14.0C, min 5.8C

Year's highest 30.4C on 16 August, lowest -8.7C on 3 December. Highest minimum 16.5C on 15 August, lowest maximum -0.5C on 18 January. Rain 486.1mm on 128 days. Wettest 47.2mm on 19 June

1974 Avg max 13.7C, min 5.9C

Year's highest 25.8C 20 June, lowest -6.7C on 1 January. Highest minimum 15.9C on 20 July, lowest maximum -0.7C on 2 January. Rain 583.3mm on 164 days. Wettest 24.3mm on 4 July.

1975 Avg max 14.7C, min 5.9C

Year's highest 33.3C on 8 August, lowest -4.1C on 14 November. Highest minimum 18.0C on 5 August, lowest maximum -0.5C on 30 November, Rain 438.3mm on 155 days, Wettest 24.6mm on 4 December.

16 snow days.

1976 Avg max 14.7C, min 5.9C

Year's highest 34.1C on 26 June, lowest -5.2C on 4,5 December. Highest minimum 17.7C on 19 July, lowest maximum -0.2C on 5 December. Rain 470.6mm on 143 days, wettest 25.8mm on 24 September 20 snow days. (S8mmer of the Century, lasted into October with six days over 21C (70F))

1977. Avg max 13.5C, min 5.8C

Year's highest 28.9C on 1 August, lowest -5.6C on 30 January. Highest minimum 16.5C on 23 July, lowest maximum -0.5C on 12 January. Rain 645.6mm on 167 days. Wettest 27.0mm on 1 November. 30 snow days.

1978 Avg max 13.2C, min 5.8C

Year's highest 29.2C on 1 June, lowest -7.4C on 1 December, Highest minimum 16.8C on 10 September, Lowest maximum -3.2C on 30 November. Rain 658.4mm on 161 days. Wettest 26.9mm on 13 August 36 snow days. (Very mild November ended with severe frost on 30th)

1979 Avg max 12.8C min 5.2C

Year's highest 28.3C on 27 July, lowest -12.2C on 28 January. Highest minimum 16.1C on 18 July, lowest maximum -3.0C on 1 January. Rain 643.8mm on 179 days. Wettest 49.1mm on 14 August, 44 snow days (very cold first three months)

1980 Avg max 13.2C, min 5.7C

Year's highest 27.7C on 4 June, lowest -6.6C on 14 January. Highest mimimum 15.9C on 15 August, lowest maximum -0.1C on 18 January. Rain 674.4 on 163 days. Wettest 49.1mm on 14 August. 18 snow days.

1981 Avg max 13.2C, min 5,5C

Year's highest 28.2C on 4,17 August, lowest -12.6C on 13 December. Highest minimum 19.3C on 9 July, lowest maximum -5.8C on 17 December. Rain 610.1mm on 178 days. 33 snow days (Coldest recorded December)

1982 Avg max 14.2C, min 6.0C

Year's highest 30.2C on 3 August, lowest -14.0C on 14 January Hgihest minimum 17.2C on 8 July, lowest maximum -4.4C on 14 January Rain 571.6mm on 158 days. Wettest 33.1mm on 22 June. 18 snow days.

1983 Avg max 14.8C, min 6.4C

Year's highest 31.7C on 15 July, lowest -6.2C on 4 February. Highest minimum 19.2C on 20 July, lowest maximum 0.8C on 10,19 February, Rain 523.5mm on 161 days, Wettest 523.5mm on 26 November. 20 snow days.

1984. Avg max 14.0C, min 6.2C

Year's highest 30.8C on 8 July, lowest -5.8C on 25 January. Highest minimum 17.0C on 2 July, lowest maximum -1.3C on 27 December. Rain 665.3mm on 164 days. Wettest 44.1mm on 2 August. 20 snow days

1985. Avg max 13.4C, min 5.7C

Year's highest 28.6C on 1 October, lowest -9.9C on 17 January. Highest minimum 18.0C on 30 July, lowest maximum -5.4C on 17 January. Rain 412.9mm on 172 days, wettest 26.1mm on 14 May. 32 snow days. (record heat on 1 October)

1986. Ave max 13.2C, min 5.0C

Year's highest 29.8C on 15 July, lowest -10.1C on 10 February. Highest minimum 15.7C on 17 June/ 16 July. Lowest maximum -1.8C on 20 February. Rain 575.6mm on 174 days. Wettest 26.1mm on 25 August, 33 snow days.

1987. Ave max 13.2C, min 5.5C

Year's highest 28.6C on 20 August, lowest -16.1C on 13 January. Highest minimum 18.1C on 29 June, lowest maximum -4.8C on 12 January, Rain 700.1mm on 169 days, wettest 30.7mm on 22 August. 25 snow days. (Record low on 13th actually occurred at about 20h on 12th)

1988. Ave max 14.1C, min 6.3C

Year's highest 30.4C on 7 August, lowest -5.0C on 22 November. Highest minimum 16.8C on 22 July, lowest maximum 2.9C on 21 November.Rain 591.5mm on 153 days, wettest 26.8mm on 20 July. 9 snow days.

1989 Ave max 15.4C, min 6.4C

Year's highest 34.3C on 22 July, lowest -3.5 on 17 February. Highest minimum 16.5C on 23 July, lowest maximum 0.8C on 27 November. Rain 550.3mm on 145 days, wettest 34.9mm on 30 June. 11 snow days.

1990 Ave max 15.6C, min 6.9C

Year's highest 37.0C on 3 August, lowest -5.1C on 5 April. Highest minimum 18.9C on 24 August, lowest maximum 1.5C on 8 December. Rain 559.8mm on 148 days, wettest 51.4mm on 17 October. 7 snow days.

1991 Ave max 14.2C, min 6.0C

Year's highest 30.5C on 1 September, lowest -10.0C on 14 February. Highest minimum 18.4C on 10 August , lowest maximum -2.7C on 12 December. Rain 430.7mm on 134 days, wettest 27.9mm on 28 September. 5 snow days.

1992 Ave max 14.3C, min 6.4C

Year's highest 30.8C on 29 June, lowest -6.7C on 22 January. Highest minimum 16.6C on 30 June, lowest maximum -2.2C on 29 December. Rain 644.4mm on 169 days. Wettest 31.0mm on 22 September, 5 snow days

1993 Ave max 13.4C, min 6.0C

Year's highest 28.1C on 9 June, lowest -6.0C on 3 January. Highest minimum 15.5C on 16 July/20 August. Lowest maximum -0.9C on 2 January. 14 snow days

1994 Ave max 14.0C, Min 6.7C

Year's highest 32.2C on 11 July, lowest -6.3C on 22 February. Highest minimum 18.0C on 27 July/5 August. Lowest maximum -1.3C on 23 December. Rain 596.4mm on 159 days, wettest 46.3mm on 14 September 12 snow days.

1995. Ave max 14.5C, Min 6.7C

Year's highest 32.2C on 1 August, lowest -7.2C on 29 December. Highest minimum 20.3C on 30 July, lowest maximum -3.0C on 28 December. Rain 475.4mm on 144 days, wettest 27.9mm on 10 September. 14 snow days.

1996. Ave max 13.1C, min 5.6C

Year's highest 31.6C on 22 July, lowest -5.1C on 26 December. Highest minimum 17.6C on 14 July, lowest maximum -1.1C on 27 January. Rain 485.8mm on 148 days, wettest 27.3mm on 19 Dec. 20 snow days.

1997 Ave max 14.8C, min 6.9C

Year's highest 32.8C on 11 August, lowest -7.7C on 3 January. Highest minimum 19.0C on 13 August, lowest maximum -0.1C on 3 January. Rain 641.8mm on 151 days, wettest 39.4mm on 11 June. 10 snow days.

1998 Ave max 13.9C, min 6.9C

Year's highest 28.7C on 10 August, lowest -3.8C on 28 January. Highest minimum 17.7C on 21 June, lowest maximum 1.3C on 21 December. Rain 809.2mm on 175 days, wettest 51.4mm on 31 July. 7 snow days

1999. Ave max 14.4C, min 8.0C

Year's highest 32.9C on 2 August, lowest -6.3C on 20 December. Highest minimum 18.7C on 3 August, lowest maximum -1.4C on 20 December. Rain 704.7mm on 168 days, wettest 52.7mm on 25 August. 11 snow days.

2000 Ave max 14.0C, min 7.3C

Year's highest 33.4C on 19 June, lowest -3.1C on 31 December. Highest minimum 17.7C on 3 August, lowest maximum 0.1C on 28 December. Rain 839.2mm on 170 days, wettest 28.4mm on 11 November. 5 snow days. (very wet autumn with severe flooding in November.)

2001. Ave max 13.9C, min 7.5C

Year's highest 31.1C on 15 August, lowest -5.1C on 18 January.Highest minimum 20.9C on 3 July, lowest maximum -1.0C on 17 January. Rain 651.4mm on 153 days, wettest 23.9mm on 14 May. 17 snow days.

2002. Ave max 14.8C, min 7.9C

Year's highest 29.8C on 17 August, lowest -6.6C on 2 January. Highest minimum 18.4C on 30 July, lowest maximum 1.2C on 4 January. Rain 724.8mm on 166 days, wettest 35.3mm on 30 July. 3 snow days.

2003. Ave max 14.7C, min 7.5C

Year's highest 30,3C on 9 August, lowest -3.8C on 31 December.Highest minimum 19.0C on 10 August. Lowest maximum 1.2C on 30 December. Rain 475.9mm on 132 days, wettest 24.8mm on 22 June. 10 snow days. (missed ou on the records highs reached further south)

2004 Ave max 14.4C, min 8.0C

Year's highest 29.5C on 8 June, lowest -2.5C on 2,3,20 December. Highest minimum 21.9C on 9 August. Lowest maximum 1.5C on 25 February. Rain 751.8mm on 172 days, wettest 98.4mm on 9 August. 11 snow days.

2005 Ave max 14.5C, min 7.7C

Year's highest 31.8C on 19 June, lowest -3.9 on 19 November. Highest minimum 18.3C on 20 June, lowest maximum -1.1C on 30 December. Rain 578.7mm on 148 days, wettest 30.7mm on 18 August. 16 snow days

2006. Ave max 14.9C, min 8.3C

Year's highest 31.8C on 19 June, lowest -5,1 on 3 March. Highest minimum 18.7C on 22 July, lowest maximum -1.9C on 30 December. Rain 627.8mm on 157 days, wettest 33.0mm on 22 July. 9 snow days.

2007 Ave max 14.6C, min 7.8C

Year's highest 28.8C on 5 August, lowest -4.4C on 7 February. Highest minimum 17.6C on 4 August, lowest maximum 1.5C on 14 December. Rain 785.2mm on 152 days, wettest 47.9mm on 22 June. 5 snow days

2008 Ave max 14.5C, min 7.4C

Year's highest 31.3C on27 July, lowest -5.0C on 18 February. Highest minimum 18.9C on 27 July/30 August, lowest maximum -0.5C on 31 December. Rain 634.3mm on 159 days, wettest 25.0mm on 5 September, 8 snow days.

2009 Ave max 14.8C, min 7.4C

Year's highest 31.5C on 1 July, lowest -5.7C on 20 December. Highest minimum 18.5C on 1 July, lowest maximum 0.1C on 10 January. Rain 572.0mm on 166 days, wettest 25.7mm on 7 June. 15 snow days

2010 Ave max 13.5C, min 6.9C

Year's highest 30.7C on 22 May, lowest -12.0C on 7 December. Highest minimum 20.0C on 2 July, lowest maximum -4.1C on 20 December. Rain 533.5mm on 160 days, wettest 23.4mm on 23 September. 33 snow days.

Coldest and Warmest Months on record.

Listed below and the coldest and warmest months on record; those below 1.0C or above 18.5C

Temperature	Month	Temperature	Month
-1.4	Jan-1963	20.6	July-2006
-0.8	Feb-1968	20	July-1995
-0.6	Dec-1981	19.9	July-1983
-0.5	Dec-2010	19.9	Aug-1997
-0.2	Jan-1979	19.7	July-1994
0.1	Feb-1969	19.6	Aug-1975
0.6	Jan-1987	19.2	Aug-1990
0.7	Feb-1956	19.2	Aug-1995
0.9	Jan-1983	19.1	July-1999
0.9	Jan-1985	19	Aug-1955
0.9	Feb-1979	19	Aug-1959
		18.8	Aug-2003
		18.7	July-1959
		18.5	July-1991
		18.5	July-2003

Decadal Temperatures graphically

Temoeratures 1951-60

■Highest Temp ◆Lowest Temp ▽Highest Min ▲Lowest Max

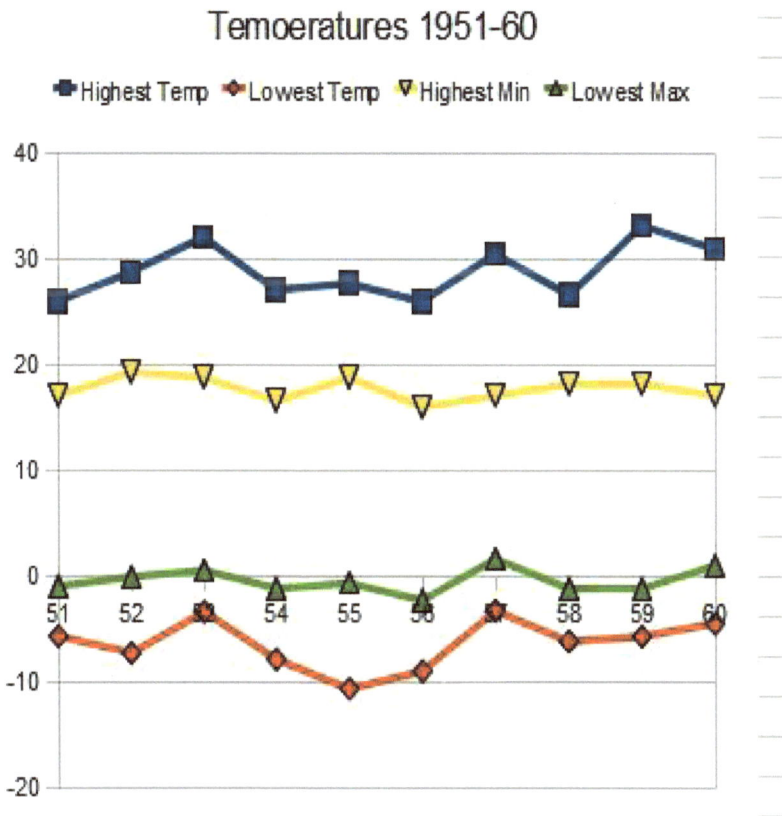

Temperatures 1961-70

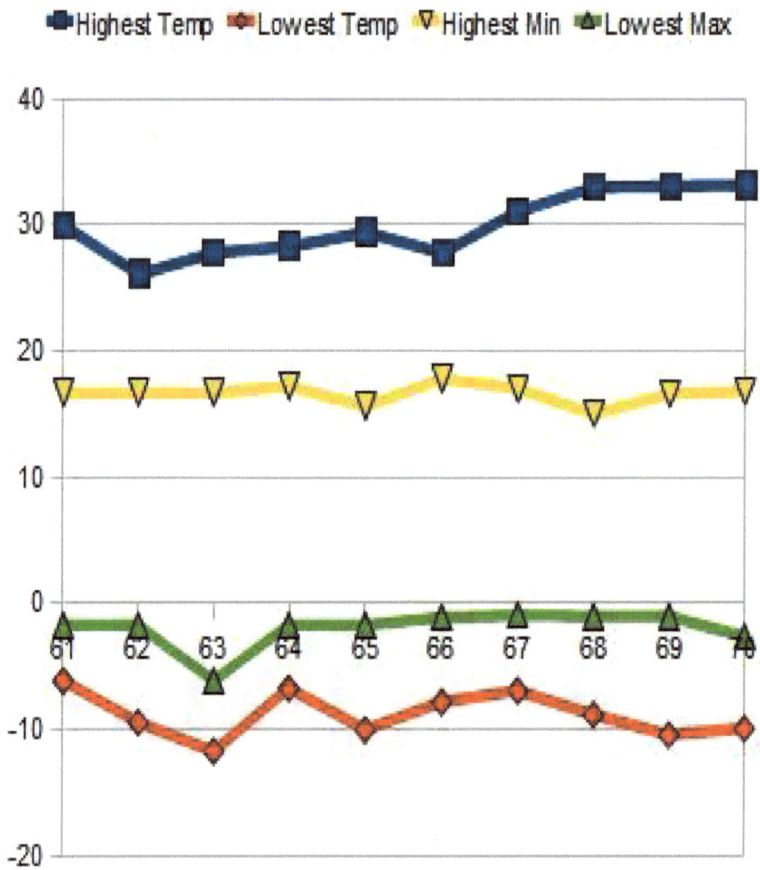

Legend: ■ Highest Temp ◆ Lowest Temp ▽ Highest Min ▲ Lowest Max

Temperature 1971-80

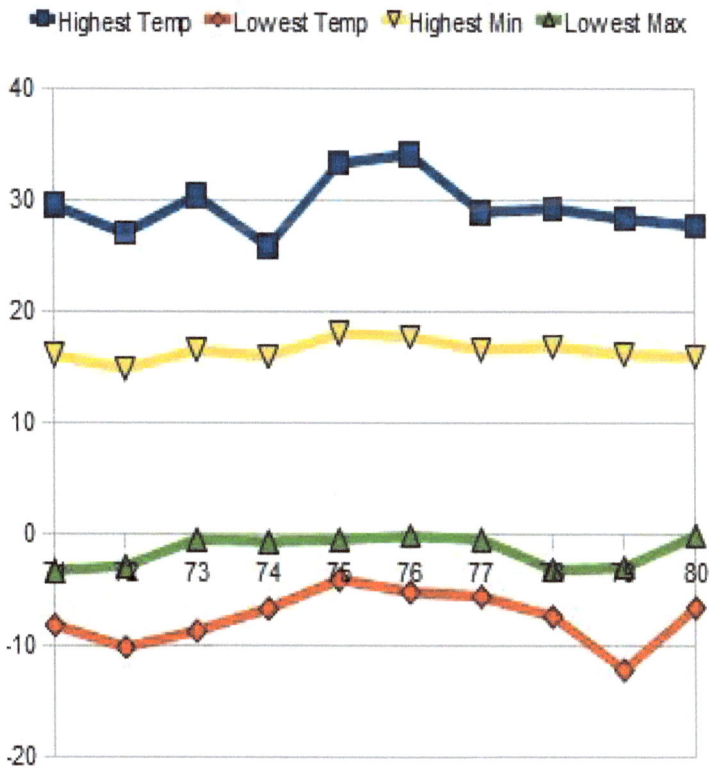

Temperatures 1981-90

■ Highest Temp ■ Lowest Temp ▽ Highest Min ▲ Lowest Max

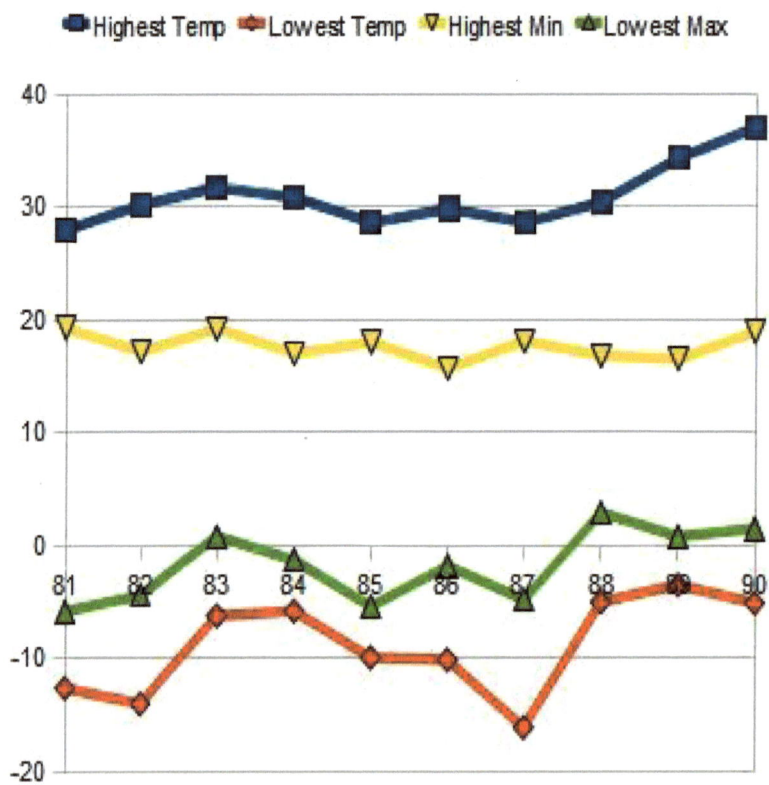

Temperatures 1991-2000

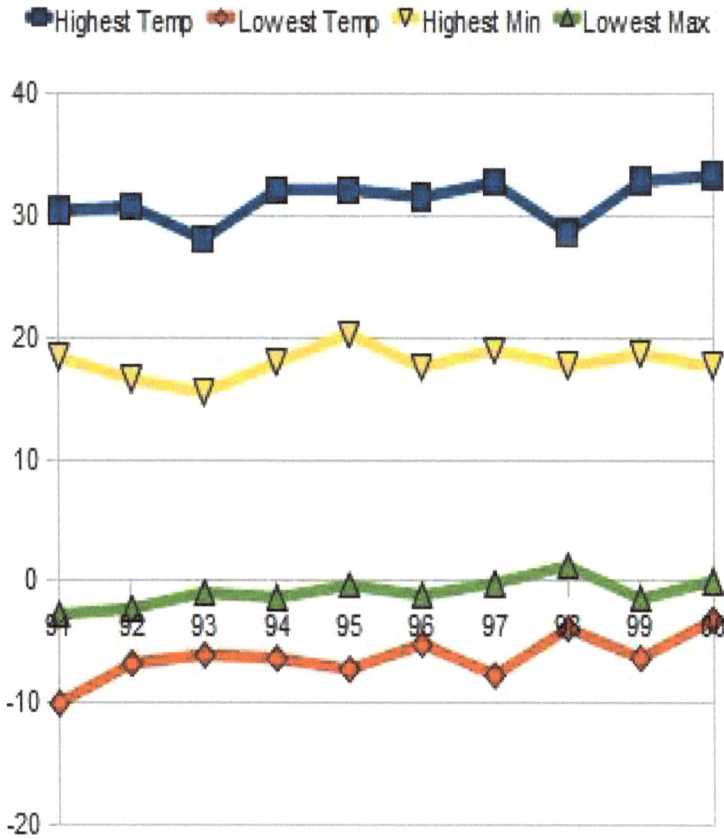

23

Temperatures 2001-10

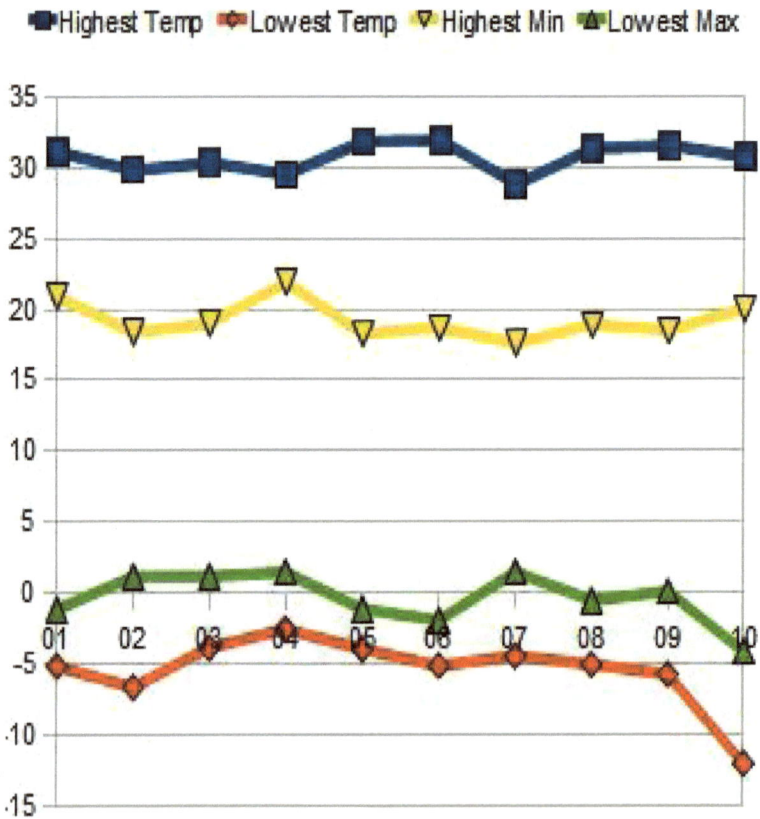

LONG-TERM TEMPERATURE* (1951-2010)

	Jan	Feb	Mar	Apr	May	June
Ave Highest	12.1	12.5	15.9	19.6	24.7	27.6
Abs Highest	14 16,1993	18.3 23,1990	23.4 29,1965	25 30,1990	30.7 23,2010	34.1 26,1976
Ave Lowest	-5.2	-5.7	-2.2	-1.2	1.9	5.2
Abs Lowest	-16.1 13,1987	-10.5 28,1955	-10 3,1965	-6.5 20,1968	-2.8 27,1967	0.9 2,1989
Ave Max	5.9	6.8	9.9	13.1	17.2	20.7
Ave Min	1.7	1.2	2.8	5.2	6.9	10.4
Air Frosts	9	10	5.4	2.3	0.3	0
Freeze Days	1.3	0.4	0	0	0	0
Warm Days**	0	0	0	0	1.1	4.5

*in degrees Celsius

**Above 25C

LONG-TERM TEMPERATURE* (1951-2010)

	July	Aug	Sep	Oct	Nov	Dec
Ave Highest	27.7	27.9	24	19.6	14.7	12.1
Abs Highest	34.3 22,1989	37 3,1990	30.5 1,1991	28.4 1,1985	17.5 2,2005	14.9 15,1982
Ave Lowest	6.5	7.3	4.4	0.6	-2.7	-4.2
Abs Lowest	4.1 12,1972	4 31,1986	-1.4 17,1986	-4.1 29,1997	-8.8 28,2010	-12.6 13,1981
Ave Max	22.3	21.8	18.7	13.9	9.1	6.7
Ave Min	12.4	12.2	10.2	7.4	4.1	2.9
Air Frosts	0	0	0	1	4.3	7.8
Freeze Days	0	0	0	0	0.3	1
Warm Days**	7.2	5.4	1	0.2	0	0

*in degrees Celsius
**Above 25C

Temperature; month-by-month graphically

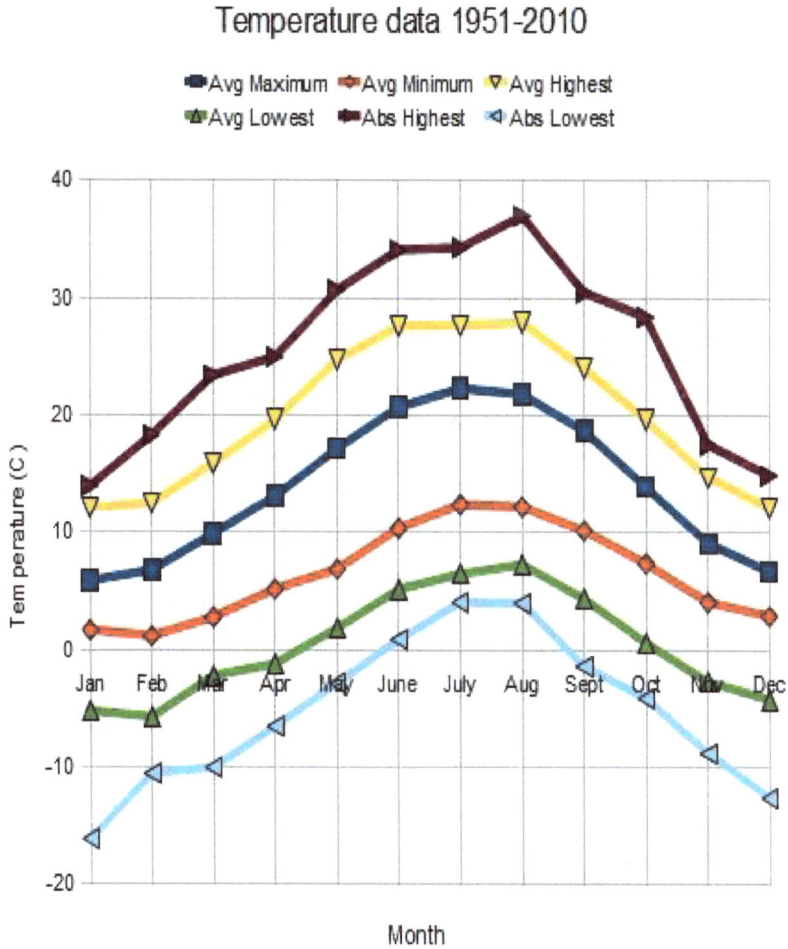

Temperature data 1951-2010

RAINFALL: THE FACTS.

Reliable rainfall data are not available before 1969, so the span of years is just 42. There is also a gap in data for the months of May to December 1993. Data are presented in millimeters. (There are 25.4mm to 1 inch rain.)

Days when snow falls are included in the total: this is standard practice. The snow collected in the guage is melted and the water thus obtained is the day's total. Rainfall has throughout been measured at 08h and the total credited to the day before (as that represented 2/3 of the day.).

Newark-on-Trent lies in the dry southeastern quarter of the country which is well away the driest.

RAINFALL DATA (1969-2010)

	Average	Wettest	Driest	Rain Days
Jan	50.2	96.1(1984)	10.4(2000)	16.4
Feb	38.5	147.4(1977)	10.1(1993)	13
Mar	41.7	87.2(1981)	9.0(1990)	14.4
Apr	42	145.7(2000)	2.9(2007)	12.8
May*	48	108.7(1983)	13.6(1991)	12.1
June*	60.3	180.6(1997)	7.3(1976)	11.2
July*	56.6	136.8(2007)	7.5(1995)	11.4
Aug*	56.4	183.2(2004)	2.2(1983)	11.5
Sep*	50.2	115.0(1976)	6.2(1986)	11.8
Oct*	51.2	125.9(2004)	16.1(1975)	13.9
Nov*	53	93.2(2002)	19.3(1978)	17
Dec*	53.1	146.0(1978)	14.7(1980)	15.6

*No data for 1993

Oustanding Months.

Below are lsited the most oustanding rainfall months. We note the months of highest and lowest rainfall toal

We note (a) the driest months; all those with a rainfall total below 8.0mm (b) the wettest months. Here we include months with above 120mm

Driest and Wettest Months on record.(mm rain)

Driest	Month	Wettest	Month
2.2	June-1983	242.7	June-2007
4.8	October-1978	183.2	August-2004
6.2	September-1986	180.6	June-1997
6.8	October-1969	151.7	June-1998
7.3	April-1974	146	December-1978
7.3	June-1976	136.8	July-2007
7.5	June-1995	135.9	July-2002
		122.8	June-1987

Rainfall data Year-by-Year graphically

Rainfall data 1969-2010

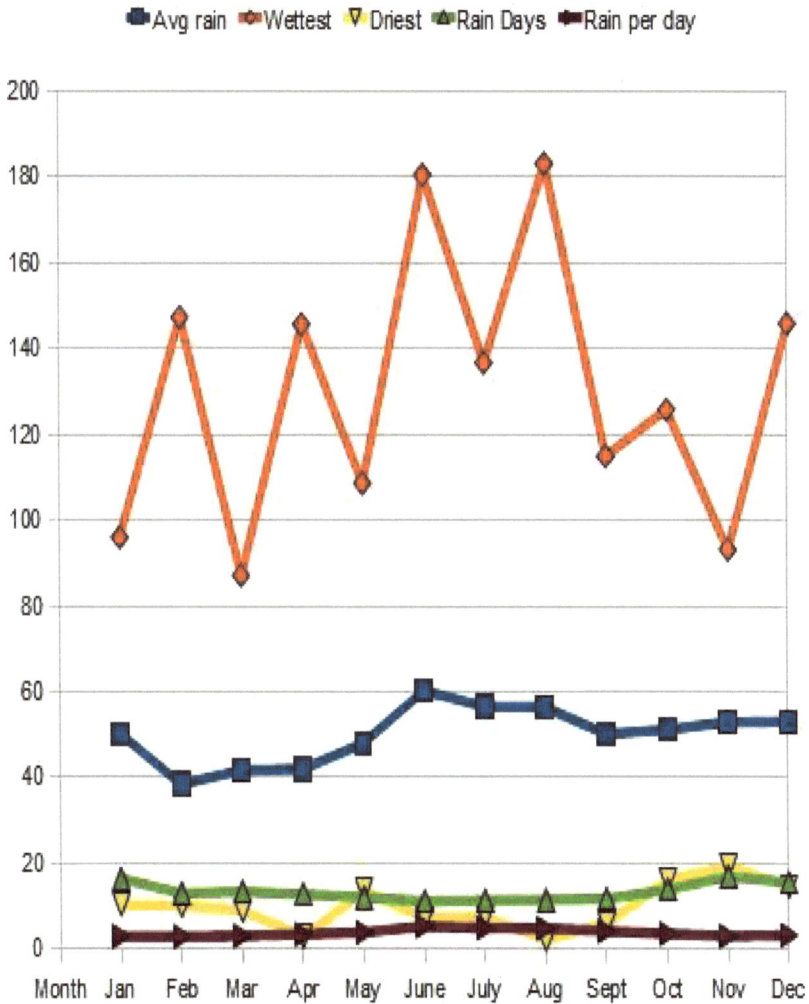

Legend: Avg rain ■ Wettest ◆ Driest ▽ Rain Days ▲ Rain per day ▶

Other data through the year:

A. Snowfall

I come to snowfall first because of its potential to affect and impact our lives. Newark has little of the disruption experienced in some other parts of the country, mainly because heavy snowfalls are rare. Only twice has more than six inches (15cm) snow fallen. In mid-February 1997 heavy falls of snow piled up 7 inches (17.5cm) snow, and with strong winds many rural parts around Newark became isolated. An even greater fall of 10 inches occurred in late November 2010, but less in the way of wind and subsequent drifting there was not the same degree of disruption.

The table below shows the number of days with snow observed to fall (this includes sleet). Days of 'snow cover' are registered when snow is observed to cover at least 50% of the surface surrounding the observing station at 09h.

	Jan	Feb	Mar	Apr	May	June	Oct	Nov	Dec
Fall	4.7	5.4	2.7	1.6	0.15	0.03	0.03	0.9	2.9
Lying*	4	3.4	0.5	1.1	0	0	0	1.2	2.1
Yrs without	1	4	9	14	n/r	n/r	n/r	24	6

*data only available from 1972

Rain and Snowfall data graphically

Rainfall data 1971-80

■ Rainfall total   ■ Rain days   □ Wettest

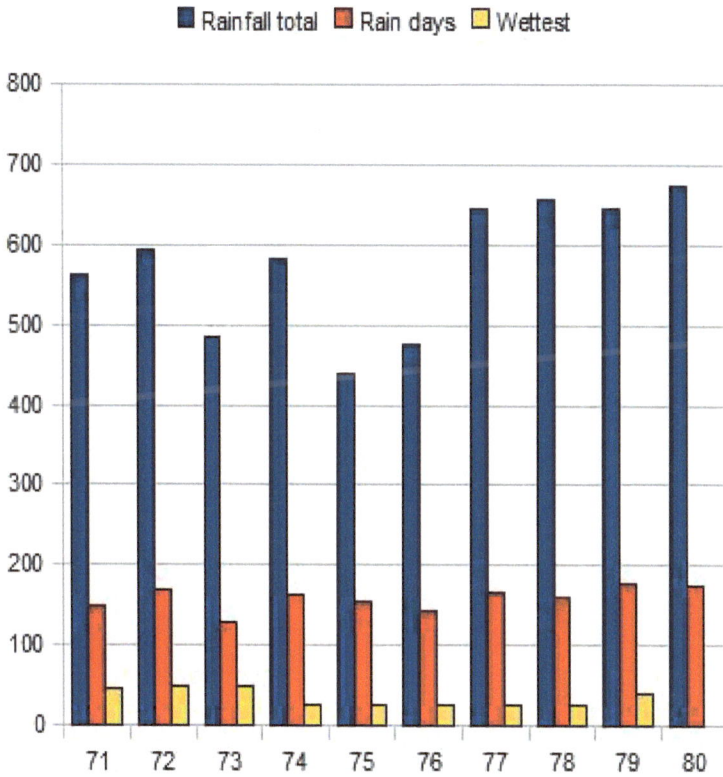

Rain & Snow 1981-90

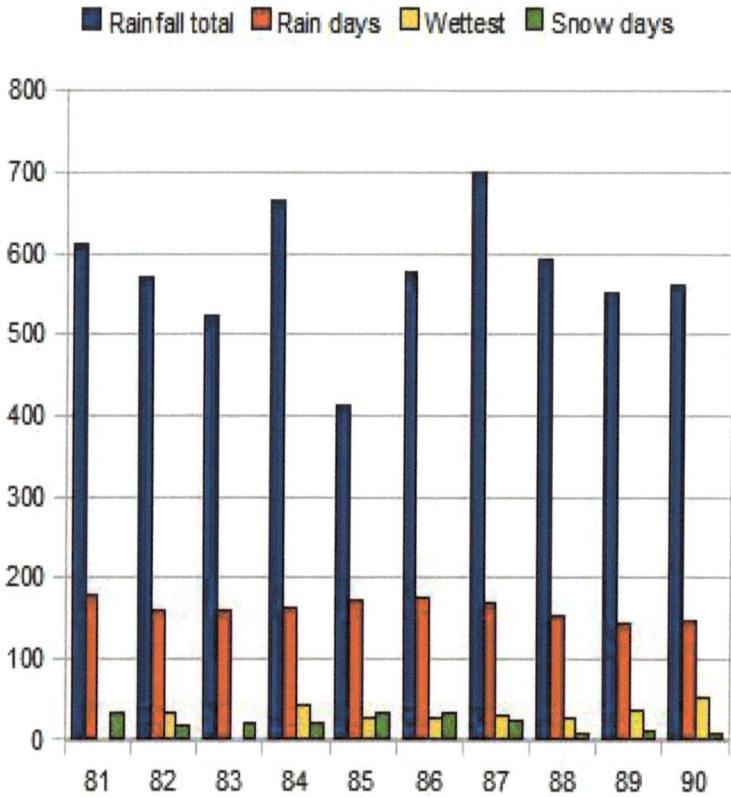

Rain & Snow 1991-2000

■ Rainfall total ■ Rain days ■ Wettest ■ Snow days

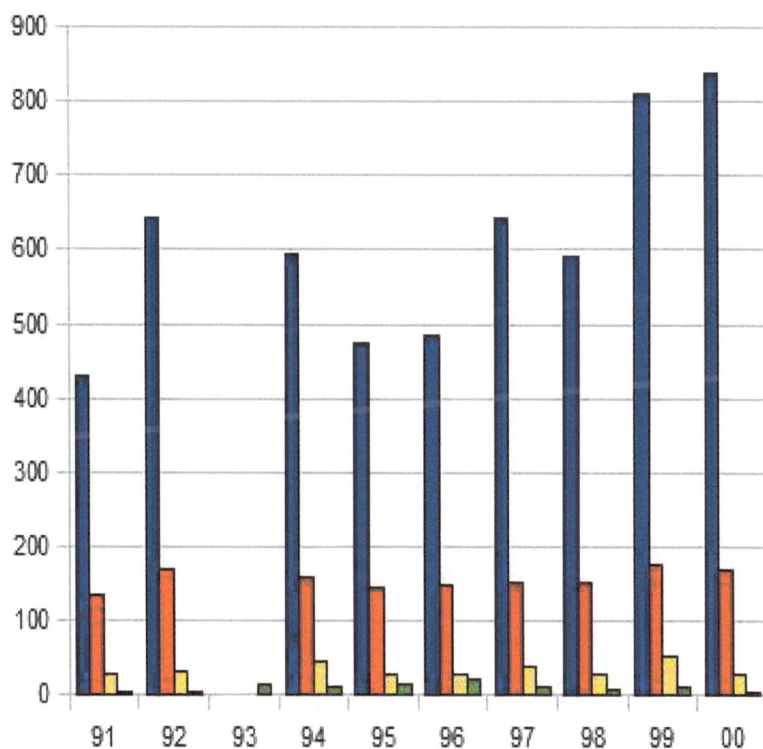

Rain & snow 2001-10

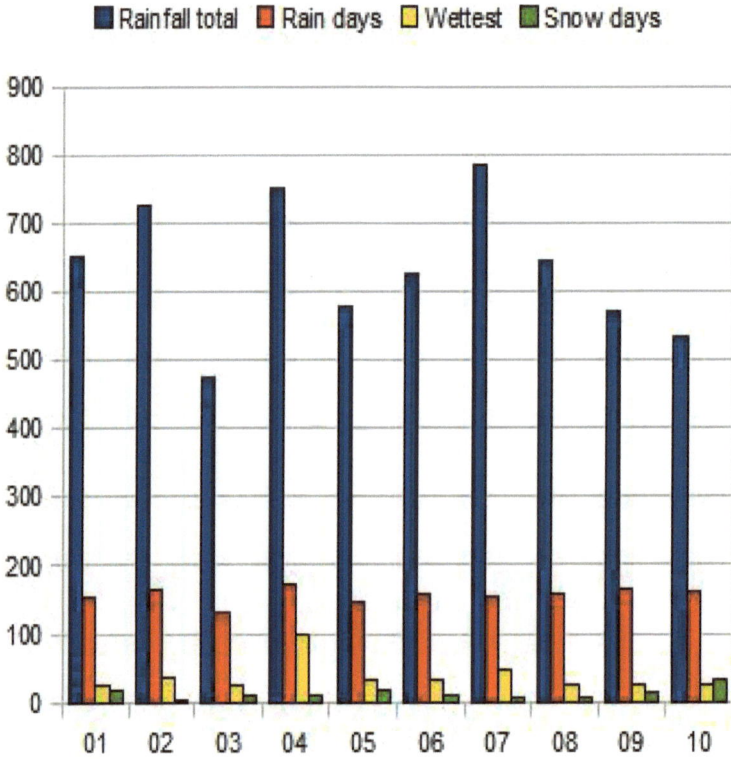

B. Frost

An air frost is recorded when the minimum temperature falls below freezing-point (-0.1C). When the maximum fails to exceed freezing-point, then this is counted as a 'freezing day'. The occurences of both elements are again presented in a month-by-month table.

'Ground Frost' is recorded when a special grass minimum thermometer laid just above the surface of grass falls below freezing-point. Whilst this element was recorded for a few years, these were too few for meaningful data to be given here.

	Jan	Feb	Mar	Apr	May	Sep	Oct	Nov	Dec
Frosts	9	10	5.4	2.3	0.3	0.05	1	4.3	7.8
Freeze Days	1.3	0.4	0	0	0	0	0	1.3	1

An interesting fact is that main winter months (January excepted) have been frost free. This occurred in December 1953, when remarkably the first frost of the winter did not occur until 1 January 1954.

Perhaps more remarkably, the February of 1961 was free of frost.

C- Fog

Fog is needless to say another element of weather which causes disruption. Many readers of this book may not have recollection of the old-fashioned 'smog'- so called because it was fog combined with smoke, and with a reduction in smoke from both domestic and industrial sources has eliminated this risk.

Fog, in the meteorological sense is recorded when the visibilty falls below 1000 metres (1 km). Fog becomes a nuisance when it, mainly, makes transport-movement difficult or dangerous. (This author recalls acting as a consultant to the Environment Agency over plans for the route of the by-pass for the A46).

Fog, again, is mainly a fact-of-life in the winter half of the year. During the summer any mist of fog which might form overnight is dispersed readily once the sun is up. It can be a hazard in coastal locations. To record 'fog', visibility of less than 1 km must be observed at 09h.

Observations of 'fog' were not kept until 1971, so we have 40 years of data to work with.

(see facing page for fog data)

D)-Hail and Thunder

These two elements need no introduction. Both products of an 'unstable' atmosphere they tend to occur together.

We should note however a type of hail known as 'soft hail'. Most hail is the result of frozen rain droplets being carried up and down by air-currents. On each ascent, the frozen drops accrete yet more ice, increasing in weight until finally the updraught can hold them no longer.

Date for fog (1971-2010)

	Days with fog (average)
January	1.1
February	1.4
March	0.6
April	0.2
May	0.05
June	0
July	0.07
August	0.1
September	0.4
October	1.1
November	1.5
December	1.8

One fact that strikes immediately is that there is a correlaion between frequency of fog and the length of the night. Fog is reported most frequently in December, with the longest nights, whilst the only fog-free month is June, with the shortest nights

Soft hail is the product of a cold atmosphere.

Data for hail and thunder (1971-2010)

	Days with hail	Days with thunder
January	0.4	0.1
February	0.5	0.1
March	1.3	0.3
April	0.9	0.3
May	0.5	1.2
June	0.3	1.6
July	0.1	1.9
August	0.1	1.8
September	0.05	0.7
October	0.2	0.3
November	0.1	0.05
Dec	0.1	0.1

Chapter Two

Outstanding Weather Events

As we look back through the records, various weather events are found. Some of these are outstanding in the public memory, though this is somewhat fickle at times and depends on personal or national circumstance.

Certain seasons, especially summer or winter, and particularly the hot summers and severe winters which visit our shores from time to time. We shall look at these, but first look at weather events in relation to outstanding days or short sequence of days.

2 June 1953

500 hPa Geopotential (gpdm) und Bodendruck (hPa)

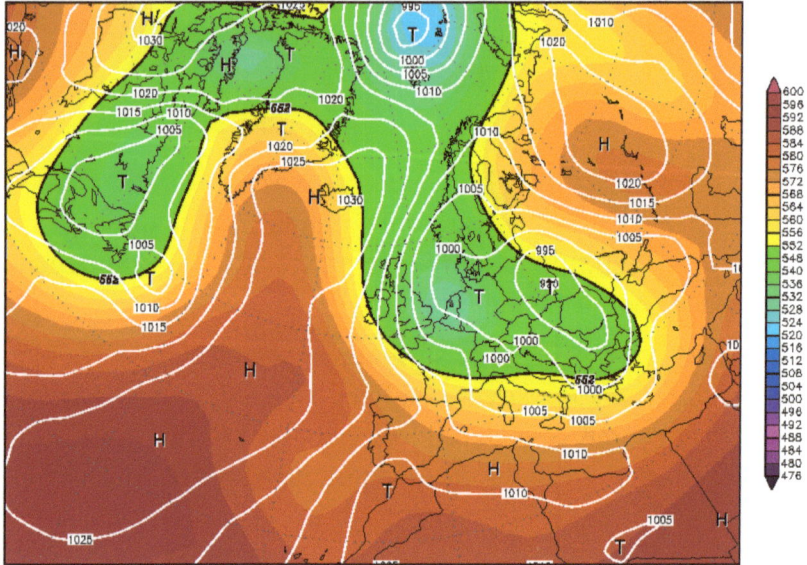

Daten: Reanalysis des NCEP
(C) Wetterzentrale
www.wetterzentrale.de

This was, of course, Coronation Day. Just a week earlier it had been hot reaching 28.5C, but very different now, with a real squeeze in the isobar, with high pressure to the west and a Low over the Continent. The day was wet, windy and cold with maximum 11.1C. It was reported that snow fell over the Scottish Highlands!

1-5 October 1959

As the hot summer of 1959 extended into autumn, so October got off to a very warm start, with southerly winds and high pressure to the east, it was fine and sunny, with all the first five days into a range 21-24.5C

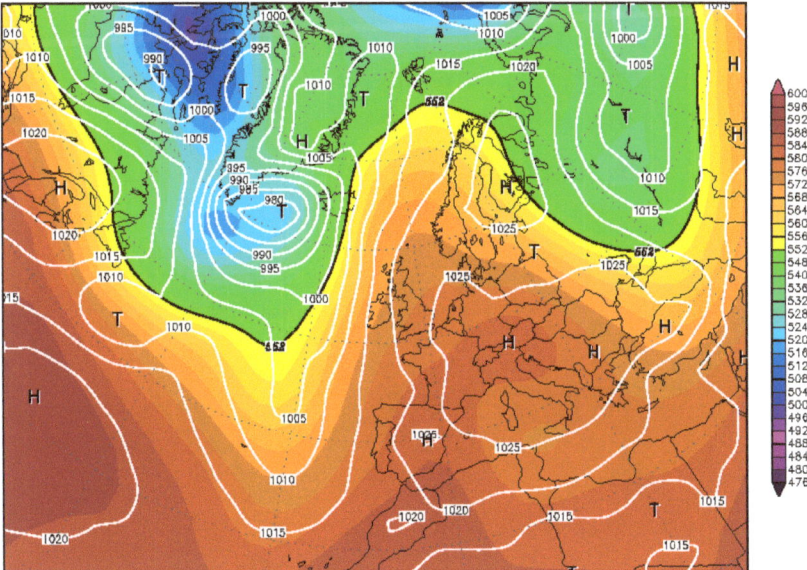

03OCT1959 00Z
500 hPa Geopotential (gpdm) und Bodendruck (hPa)

Daten: Reanalysis des NCEP
(C) Wetterzentrale
www.wetterzentrale.de

21-25 January 1963:

1962-3 was the coldest winter of the record: in fact it had the lowest CET* since 1740. The most severe spell was from 21-25 January. Just as it seemed the severe cold might be ameliorating, a fresh burst of easterly winds behind a deepening low which plunged south across the country brought heavy snowfall on the 21st. The 22nd was brilliantly sunny with a bitter wind. The following night under clear skies the coldest night of the winter -11.6C followed and despite sunny skies the day following could only reach -4.4C. Fog formation restricted the overnight low to -10.6C but fog held the maximum to a perishing -5.6C. Thereafter temperatures began a slow recovery

*Central England Temperature

22JAN1963 00Z
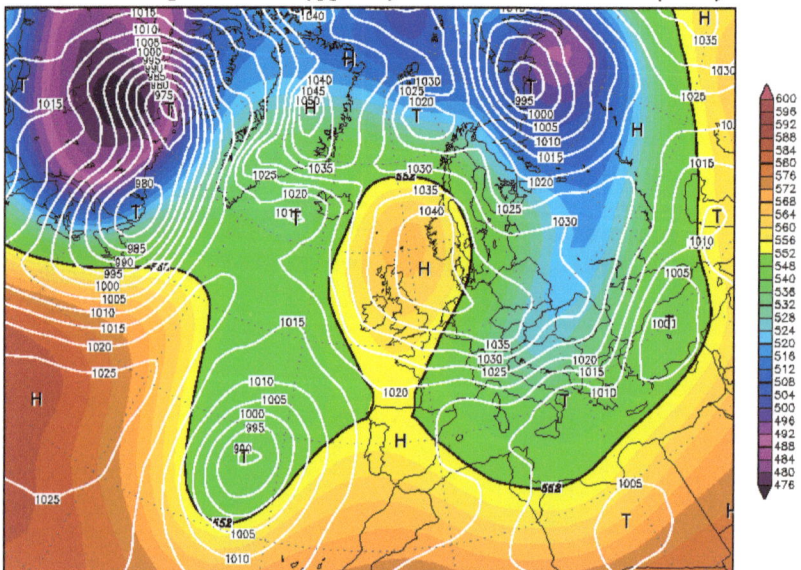
500 hPa Geopotential (gpdm) und Bodendruck (hPa)

Daten: Reanalysis des NCEP
(C) Wetterzentrale
www.wetterzentrale.de

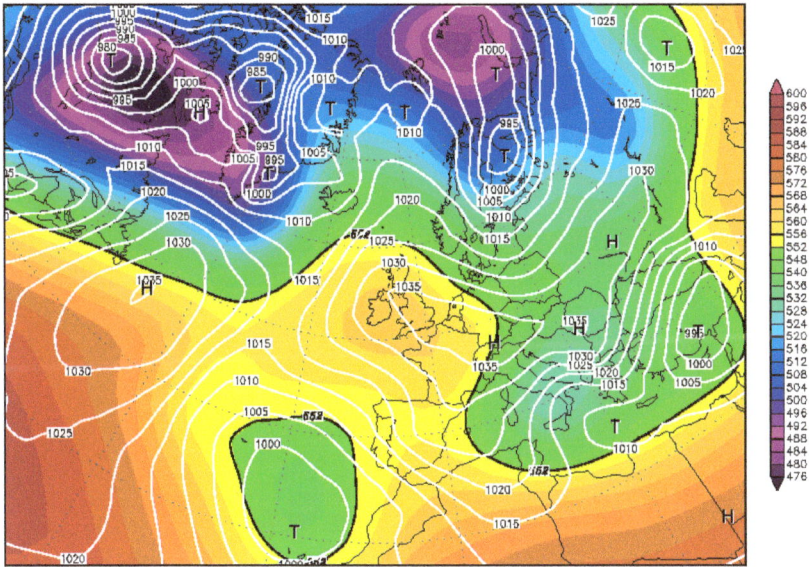

24JAN1963 00Z
500 hPa Geopotential (gpdm) und Bodendruck (hPa)

Daten: Reanalysis des NCEP
(C) Wetterzentrale
www.wetterzentrale.de

29 March 1965

At the end of a month of contrasts (It began with harsh frosts- down on the 2nd to -10C and then a more changeable period, pressure rose in an open warm sector on the 28th. The night following fell to just 1.4C But with unbroken sunshine and a low-level inversion there was an unprecedented rise in temperature to reach 23.4C- a March record.

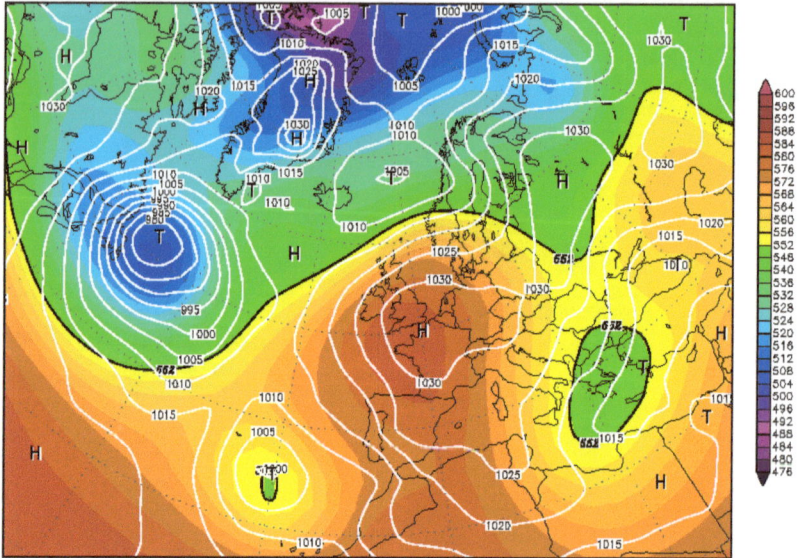

29MAR1965 00Z
500 hPa Geopotential (gpdm) und Bodendruck (hPa)

Daten: Reanalysis des NCEP
(C) Wetterzentrale
www.wetterzentrale.de

1 July 1968

In what was generally a poor summer, a 'Spanish Plume'
brought a sudden rise in temperature, to reach 33.4C on 1
July. The air which reached us originated from Saharan Africa
resulted in exceptional deposits of sand over southeastern
Britain.

500 hPa Geopotential (gpdm) und Bodendruck (hPa)

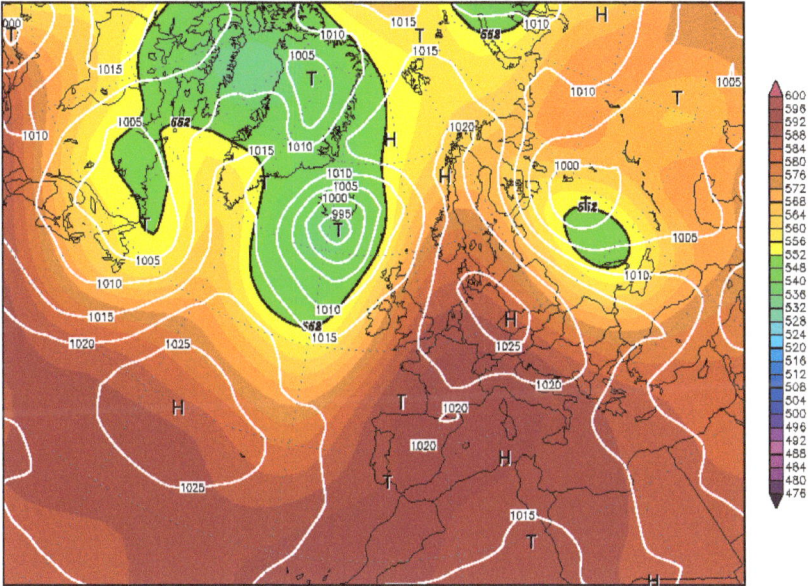

Daten: Reanalysis des NCEP
(C) Wetterzentrale
www.wetterzentrale.de

2 June 1975

A fine May had ended with high pressure retreating
northwards and a burst of cold NE winds. There was a large
reservoir of very cold air in the Arctic north of Iceland. Late
on the 1st a polar low formed near Iceland and ran south-
eastward.. Under clear skies the thermometer dropped to 2.0C,
and as the low neared it produced a heavy shower of sleet and
snow.

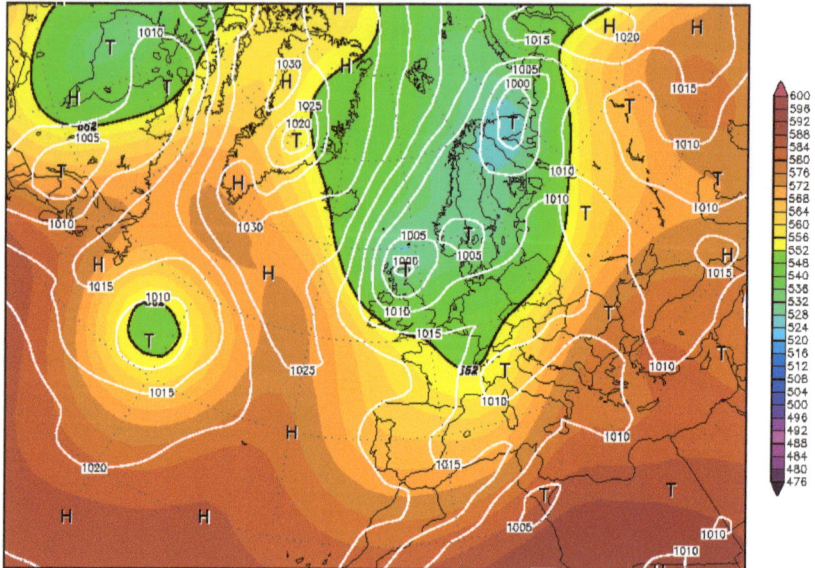

02JUN1975 00Z
500 hPa Geopotential (gpdm) und Bodendruck (hPa)

Daten: Reanalysis des NCEP
(C) Wetterzentrale
www.wetterzentrale.de

26 June 1976

This hottest June day on record came at the end of a week of
rising temperatures, reaching 34.1C, with the following day
only marginally less ho, at 33.7C. The heat developed after a
dry spring and the heat of the mid-summer sun was not used
on drying out surfaces, but fully on raising daytime
temperatures.

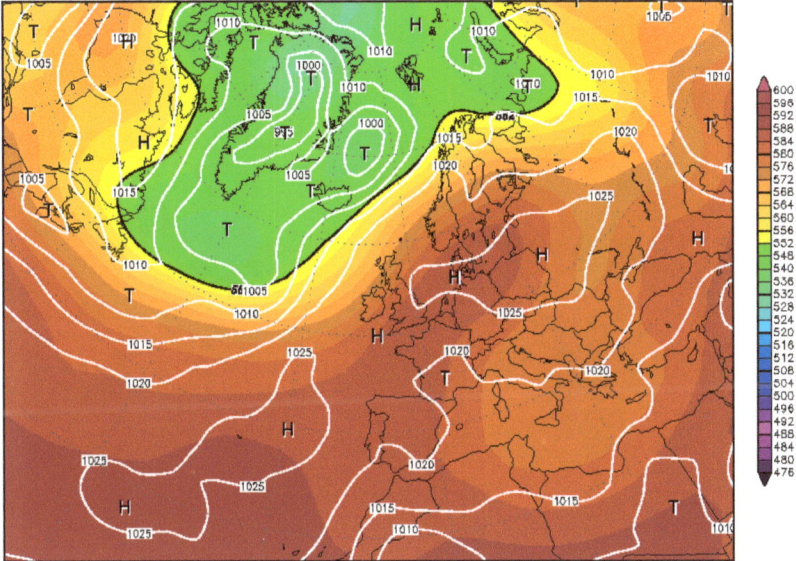

26JUN1976 00Z
500 hPa Geopotential (gpdm) und Bodendruck (hPa)

Daten: Reanalysis des NCEP
(C) Wetterzentrale
www.wetterzentrale.de

15 February 1979

1978-79 was one of the snowiest winters of the record (although less so than 1946-47). The heaviest fall occurred on 14 February. Newark received 6 inches level snow and accompanying strong winds led to severe drifting. Many villages around Newark were cut off for several days. The ferocity of the storm can be adjudged by the fact that for many hours falling snow reduced visibility to less than 100m. The day maximum was -2.7C

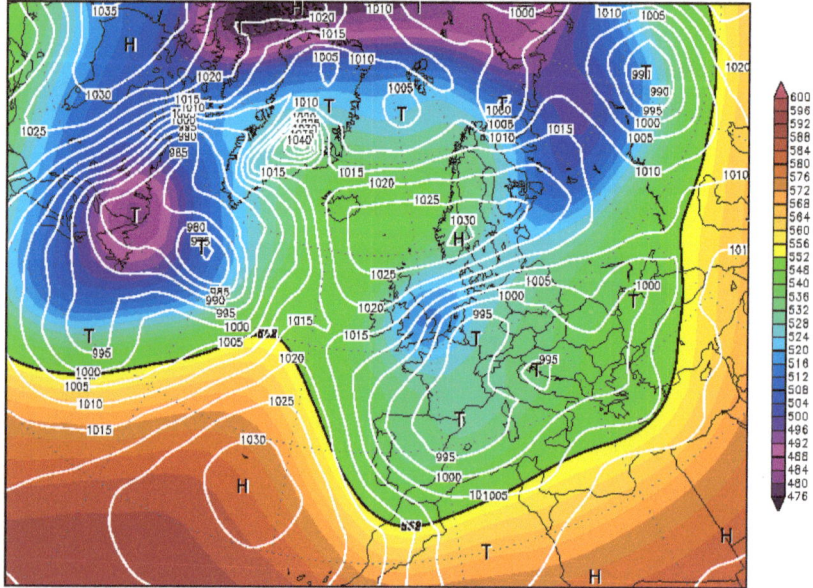

15FEB1979 00Z
500 hPa Geopotential (gpdm) und Bodendruck (hPa)

Daten: Reanalysis des NCEP
(C) Wetterzentrale
www.wetterzentrale.de

1 October 1985

This was the remarkable coda to an indifferent summer. The last week of September had produced a prolonged Indian Summer with gentle southerly breezes and day maxima of 22-24C. As the high moved away freshening southerly breezes brought air from far south. The day began with an overnight low of 17.0C, and by 08h it had already climbed to 21C. The afternoon maximum was 28.6C- the hottest day of the year

01OCT1985 00Z

500 hPa Geopotential (gpdm) und Bodendruck (hPa)

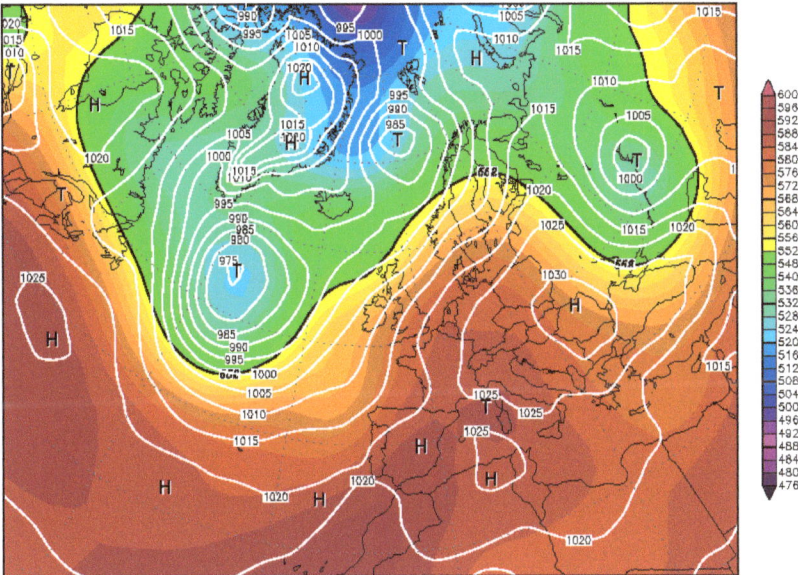

Daten: Reanalysis des NCEP
(C) Wetterzentrale
www.wetterzentrale.de

3 August 1990.

This was 'hot Friday'. High pressure to the east had produced sunny weather with steadily climbing temperatures all week. It culminated in what was for many places the hottest day on record. Newark reached a staggering 37.0C (98.6F)

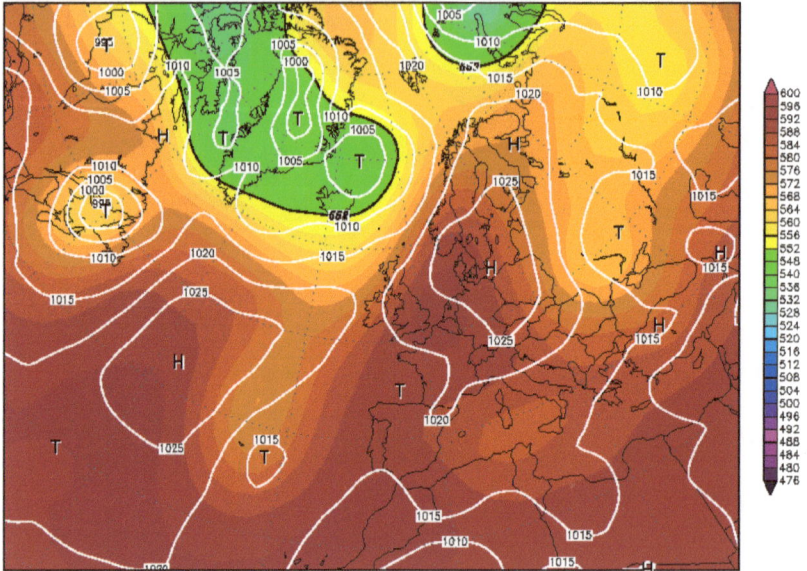

03AUG1990 00Z
500 hPa Geopotential (gpdm) und Bodendruck (hPa)

Daten: Reanalysis des NCEP
(C) Wetterzentrale
www.wetterzentrale.de

9 August 2004

In a summer of repeated heavy rainstorms, the one which occurred on the 9th August was record breaking. The preceding days had been mostly warm and sunny, then an old hurricane approached winds backed SE on the 8th which reached 29.1C. Rain began to fall at 08h on the 9th and did not finally cease until 12h on the 10th. In that period, 107.8mm rain fell, of which 98.4mm during the 'rainfall day' of the 9th. The culprit was a small but deep Low west of Ireland, and in its circulation a stationary front.

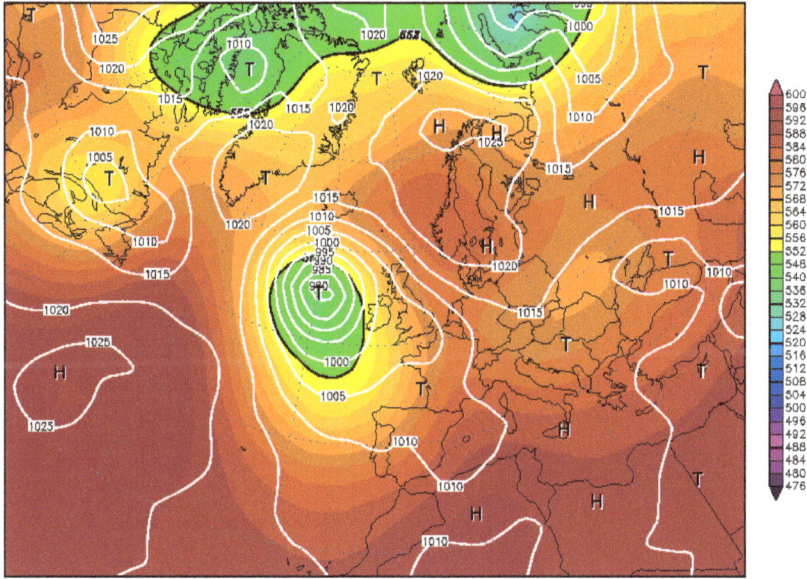

09AUG2004 00Z
500 hPa Geopotential (gpdm) und Bodendruck (hPa)

Daten: Reanalysis des NCEP
(C) Wetterzentrale
www.wetterzentrale.de

28 November 2010

The early part of November 2010 had been mild, but north-
easterlies spread across the UK on 22nd and it became
progressively colder. There had been snow early on the 27th
leaving a 2cm cover, with further snow showers during the
day. As winds fell light and skies cleared, an exceptionally
cold night followed, with a record low for November of -8.8C

28NOV2010 00Z

500 hPa Geopotential (gpdm) und Bodendruck (hPa)

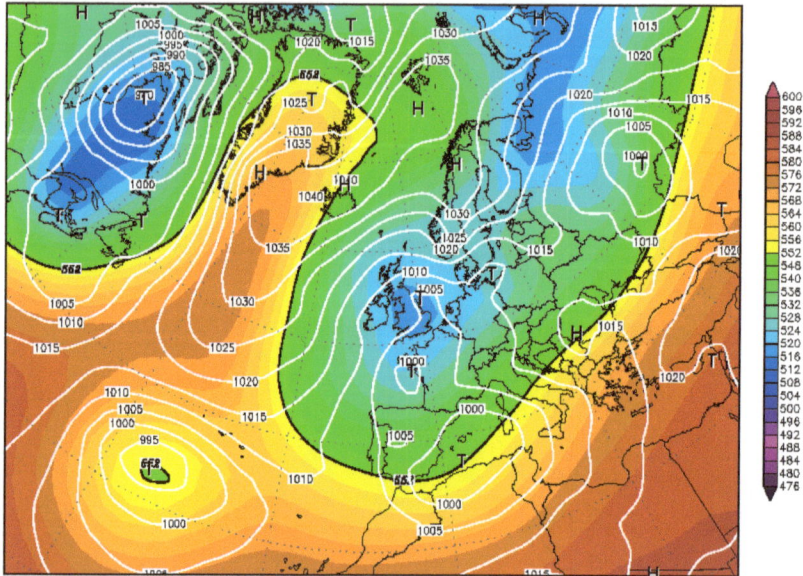

Daten: Reanalysis des NCEP
(C) Wetterzentrale
www.wetterzentrale.de

Outstanding Seasons.

There have been two classic summers and two winters which outstrip all ohers in the record in terms of sustained, respectively, of heat or cold. The summers were the succesive seasons of 1975 and 1976; the winters those of 1963 and 1979. Others summers in the 1990s run them close, especially 1990 and 1995.

Some recent winter seasons have been unusually mild and lacking 'real' winter weather. There have also been some very poor summers, notably 1956 and 1962. The recent very wet summer of 2007 was quite warm and does not compare with those earlier ones. Some of this may well be due to climatic changes. As I began to give thought to this book, the unusual cold and snow of December 2010 gave me to think that we might be in for a winter to rival 1963 and 1979, but as I write this in late January 2011 it is clear that this is not the case. So, on to consider first the hot summers, then winters,

The summers of 1975 and 1976 and the drought of 1975-6

The years 1975-76 were notable for a historic drought, and both years for remarkable summers. Over England and Wales as a whole, the summer of 1975 was one of the six warmest of the 20th century, but it was eclipsed by the summer of 1976, which in terms of the 'Central England Temperature' was the warmest since at least 1826. Of individual months, August 1975 had a mean maximum of 26.3C, whilst the value for July 1976 was 26.8C.

In both summers, one of the most notable features was the occurrence of a spell of heat notable for its intensity and duration. The 1976 major heat-wave was the more outstanding lasting from 22 June to 10 July, during which 26.5C (80F) was reached every day. The spell from 27 July to 14 August was almost as outstanding, and 26.5C was reached every day during the first two weeks of August. During the main summer months (July/August), there were 28 days over 25C in 1975 and 39 in 1976. The hottest day of 1975 reached 32.2C whilst 33.5C was surpassed on three days in 1976 (of these two were in June-see above).

The synoptic bases of both summers was a predominance of anticyclonic weather combined with advection of hot Continental air over dry ground; this was a particular factor of the 1976 heat-wave. The major heat-wave of 1975 began with the advection of Tropicl Maritime air, followed by intense anticyclonic conditions, followed by the arrival of hot Continental air..

The other feature of 1975-76 was the drought with a prolonged sequence of dry months.

(see opposite for a table of month-by-month data)

The winters of 1962-3 and 1978-9

Whilst the winter of 1962-3 was the most severe recorded and generally agreed to have been the most severe in Britain since 1739-40, that of 1978-9 was almost as severe in terms of combined cold and snowiness.

In 1963 there were cold spells in mid-November when the first snow of the season occurred and in early December daytime maxima as low as -1C were recorded, the main cold spell began (quite abruptly) on 22 December and did not remit until the final thaw on 4 March. The mean temperature for the months December to February was only -0.2C, and January and February equalled each other in the number of snow-days

The data for 1975-76 drought.

	Rain total	Rain % of normal
1975 May	39.9	84
June	9.7	20
July	48.5	84
August	33.5	55
September	49	100
October	16	38
November	37.4	66
December	44.2	86
1976 January	44.9	91
February	13	28
March	17.5	42
April	12.2	30
May	47.8	100
June	7.4	15
July	48.5	84
August	8.9	15

(16) and air frosts (23). During these months, 4,5C (40F) was reached only once (26 January), this coming at the end of the coldest ten-day period on record. From 16 January to 25

February mean maxiimum was -1.6C and mean minimum was -6.7C.

In 1979 there was no comparable cold spell. The mean for December to February was 1.1C. January had 15 snow days, and February 22 air frosts. The main cold spells were December 30- January 6; January 18-30 (a record low of -12.2C was recorded on January28) and February 9-21. This latter spell produced an exceptional blizzard with 17cm snow accumulating by February 15, which was also the coldest February day on record- maximum -2.7C

CLIMATIC TRENDS
(short- and long-term)

Climatologists now accept that our climate is warming world-wide. What is the evidence in the Newark record? The two graphs below illustrate the year-on-year records: the first graph for rainfall from 1956 through to 2005; the latter the temperature record from 1956 to 2005(shown in red). In both cases the trends are more clearly seen by the 9-year-centred moving means (shown in green)

The rainfall is shown first. It is often said that for the UK warming will also mean increased rainfall. The 9-year centred data show random year-to-year factors at play until the early 1990s, since when there has been a steady rise by 8 percent Undoubtedly temperature has also increased during the last 20 years.. The facts, as presented graphically speak for themselves.

There are also suggestions that seasonal patterns may be changing in response to global warming. There have been marked fluctuations to the seasonal distribution of rainfall, with the first five months (except April) showing reduced rainfall, but from June on a marked increase.

NB

The illustrations are based on data prepared in 2009. Note that 2010 was the coldest year since 1986, and there are suggestions that warming may be slowing down in our part of the world.

Graphical Illustration

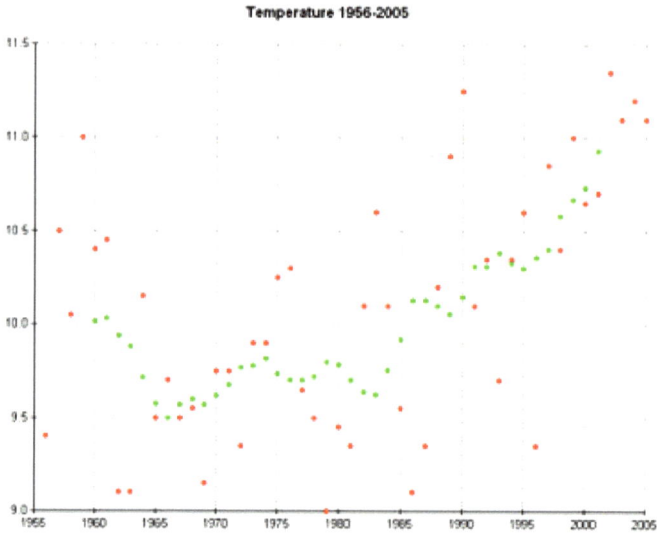

Temperature 1956-2005

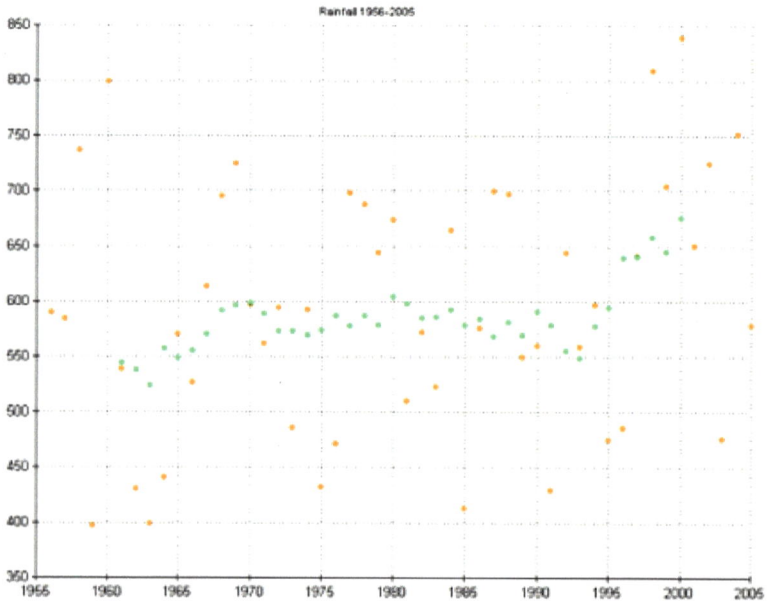

Rainfall 1956-2005

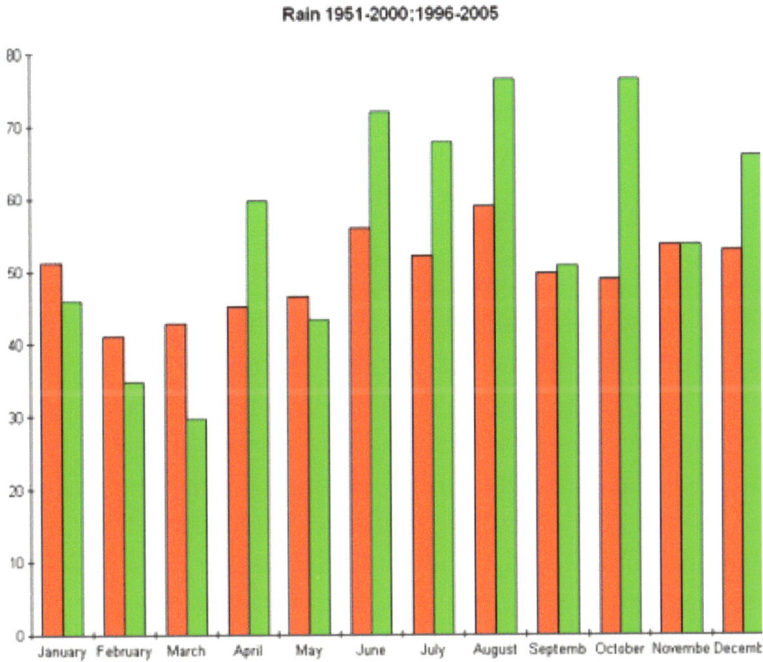

Rain 1951-2000;1996-2005

It is also to be noted that even at the decadal level, climatic change is a more variable factor. The table below lists mean annual temperature for each of the six decades covered by this book.

Decade	Decadal Avg Mean
1951-60	10.1
1961-70	9.6
1971-80	9.7
1981-90	10
1991-2000	10.3
2001-10	11.1

We see, then, that climatic warming has been very much a factor of the last two decades. These have been decades of, mainly, very mild winters, and summers which, if not always fine and sunny have at least been mild. Thus, we have already noted the fact that the 'poor' summer of 2007 was in fact warm.

The weather of 2010 has caused many to stop and pause and think on the subject of global warming. Not least have been the last three winters. After an unremarkable December and January in 2007-8, bitterly cold easterly winds swept in from Siberia at the end of January and this very cold and snowy weather lasted through to mid-February. It was long enough since, even in the collective memory, we had experienced a sustained spell of cold, snow and the attendant disruption. Just a blip maybe?

Then we had a rude shock. A week before Christmas 2009 we again experienced an incursion of cold north-easterlies with snow causing disruption. Again it lasted, and just when a thaw seemed to be setting in in the New Year, northerly winds brought more snow and frost; this lasted most of January. February was about normal, but with unwanted reminders of cold and snow. Even earlier, it all happened again in late November 2010, and we had one of the coldest Decembers on record.

Is something significant happening...? Too early to tell yet, but theories based on a decline in the Gulf Stream come to mind.

APPENDIX

Appendix One:Year-on-Year.

This work would be incomplete without a year-on-year summary of temperature and rainfall, which is presented in tabular form

	Avg Max	Avg Min	Highest	Lowest	Rainfall	Wettest
1951	13	6.3	26.1	-5.6	-	-
1952	13.2	6.3	28.9	-7.2	-	-
1953	13.9	7.1	32.2	-3.3	-	-
1954	13.3	6.5	27.2	-7.8	-	-
1955	13.5	6.3	27.8	-10.6	-	-
1956	12.8	6	26.1	-8.9	-	-
1957	13.9	7.1	30.6	-3.3	-	-
1958	13.3	6.8	26.7	-6.1	-	-
1959	15	7	33.3	-5.6	-	-
1960	13.8	7	31.1	-4.4	-	-
1961	14.1	6.8	30	-6.1	-	-
1962	12.6	5.6	26.1	-9.4	-	-
1963	12.5	5.7	27.8	-11.7		
1964	13.5	6.8	28.3	-6.7		
1965	13.3	5.7	29.4	-10		

1966	13.4	6	27.8	-6.7	-	-
1967	13.2	5.8	31.1	-6.9	-	-
1968	13.5	5.6	33	-8.8	-	-
1969	12.8	5.4	33.1	-10.4	734.6	-
1970	13.8	5.7	33.2	-9.9	597.4	43.4
1971	13.8	5.7	29.5	-8.2	562.3	46.1
1972	13.2	5.5	27	-10.2	593.7	47.8
1973	14	5.8	30.4	-8.7	486.1	47.2
1974	13.7	5.4	25.8	-6.7	563.3	24.3
1975	14.6	5.9	33.3	-4.1	438.3	24.6
1976	14.7	5.9	34.1	-5.2	470.6	25.8
1977	13.5	5.8	28.9	-5.6	645.6	27
1978	13.2	5.8	29.2	-7.4	658.4	35.8
1979	12.8	5.2	28.3	-12.2	648.3	25.9
1980	13.2	5.7	27.7	-6.6	674.4	49.1
1981	13.2	5.5	28.2	-12.6	610.1	32.4
1982	14.2	6	30.2	-14	571.6	33.1
1983	14.8	6.4	31.7	-6.3	523.5	22.6
1984	14	6.2	30.8	-5.8	665.3	44.1
1985	13.4	5.7	28.6	-9.9	412.9	26.1
1986	13.2	5	29.8	-10.1	575.6	26.1
1987	13.2	5.5	28.6	-16.1	700.1	30.7
1988	15.4	6.4	30.4	-5	591.5	26.8
1989	15.4	6.4	34.3	-3.5	550.3	34..9

1990	15.6	6.9	37	-5.1	559.8	51.4
1991	14.2	6	30.5	-10	430.7	27.9
1992	14.3	6.4	30.8	-6.7	644.4	31
1993	13.4	6	28.1	-6	-	-
1994	14	6.7	32.3	-6.3	596.4	46.3
1995	14.5	6.7	32.1	-7.2	475.4	27.9
1996	13.1	5.6	31.6	-5.1	485.8	27.3
1997	14.8	6.9	32.3	-7.7	641.9	39.4
1998	13.9	6.9	28.7	-3.8	809.2	51.4
1999	14.5	7.5	32.9	-6.3	704.7	52.7
2000	14	7.3	33.4	-3.2	839.2	28.4
2001	13.9	7.5	31.1	-5.1	651.4	23.9
2002	14.8	7.9	29.8	-6.6	724.8	35.3
2003	14.7	7.5	30.3	-3.8	475.9	24.8
2004	14.4	8	29.5	-2	751.8	98.4
2005	14.6	7.7	31.8	-3.9	578.5	30.7
2006	14.9	8.3	30.9	-5.1	627.8	33
2007	14.6	7.8	29.8	-4.4	643.3	47.9
2008	14.5	7.4	31.3	-5.6	634.3	25
2009	14.8	7.4	31.5	-5.7	572	25.7
2010	13.5	6.9	30.7	-12	533.6	23.4

Appendix 2: Photographs

A collection of weather-related photographs in Newark-on-Trent.

Note: Those presented are from the digital age, to assure quality.

This spectacular shot of a rainbow, looking across Mill Lane

SNOW PHOTOGRAPHS

3 December 2010, crystal clear, frosty early morning

Below: the same morning, low sunlight through archway, Milgate.

Easter Snow: early Easter Day 2008

Devon Park, Riverside in winter (1967)

FLOOD PHOTOGRAPHS

Frequent heavy downpours in July 2007 led to flooding at an unusual time of the year.

15th July 2007

Floods on the Trentside footpath, just south of Longstone Bridge, and (below) alongside the path

And, lastly, overleaf, sunsets.

Appendix C- useful websites and further reading:

http://newarkweather.lyall-web.co.uk/

(my Newark-on-Trent weather website)

http://uk.weather.com/weather/almanac-UKXX0887

(almanac-Newark)

http://www.uwsp.edu/geo/faculty/ritter/geog101/textbook/climate_systems/urban_climate.html

(urban climate)

http://ec.europa.eu/clima/sites/campaign/what/climatechange_en.htm

(climate change)

http://www.weatheronline.co.uk/reports/philip-eden/Snowiest-of-20th-century.htm

(December 1981)

http://www.weatheronline.co.uk/reports/philip-eden/Coronation-Weather.htm

(Coronation weather 1953)

http://www.colweather.org.uk/coltext.html

(COL-Climatological Observers' Link)

http://onlinelibrary.wiley.com/journal/10.1002/(ISSN)1477-8696

('Weather' Magazine)

http://www.weatherwise.org/

('Weatherwise' magazine)

Reading

Collin's New Natuarlist Library (115)-Climate and Weather,

Collins, September 2010, ISBN 978-0007185023 pbk £30

Atmosphere and Weather by Terry Jennings

Evans and Brothers Ltd, June 2005, ISBN 978-0237527464, £13.99

The Rough Guide to Climate Change

Rough Guides, January 2008, ISBN 978-1858281056 , £10.99

A personal note:

I was for many years a Fellow of the Royal Meteorological Society, and for 1975-78 a member of its Council. From 1967 for some 15 years I had letters and papers published in the Society's magazin 'Weather'. I list these below.

Lyall, I. T. (1967) April warmth: A predictor for the coming summer? Weather, 22, pp. 162-163.
Lyall, I. T. (1967) Dates of severe winter weather and a probable turning point in the English winter. Weather, 22, pp. 260. [LETTER]
Lyall, I. T. (1969) Which way Weather? Weather, 24, pp. 239. [LETTER, WEATHER MAGAZINE]
Lyall, I. T. (1970) Cold Christmases. Weather, 25, pp. 562. [LETTER]
Lyall, I. T. (1970) Low minima in southern Britain. Weather, 25, pp. 286. [LETTER]
Lyall, I. T. (1970) May and biennial oscillation. Weather, 25, pp. 237. [LETTER]
Lyall, I. T. (1970) Recent trends in spring weather. Weather, 25, pp. 163-165. [CLIMATE]
Lyall, I. T. (1971) Climatic periodicities. Weather, 26, pp. 41. [LETTER, STATISTICS]
Lyall, I. T. (1971) Dates of the seasons. Weather, 26, pp. 274-275. [LETTER]
Lyall, I. T. (1971) Early warm spells since 1957. Weather, 26, pp. 46-54. [CLIMATOLOGICAL REVIEW]
Lyall, I. T. (1971) English winters since 1950. Weather, 26, pp. 445-448. [CLIMATE]
Lyall, I. T. (1971) An exceptionally warm day in January. Weather, 26, pp. 541- 545

Lyall, I. T. (1971) What is a foehn? Weather, 26, pp. 548-549. [LETTER, MOUNTAIN WEATHER, WIND]

Lyall, I. T. (1972) English winters. Weather, 27, pp. 40. [LETTER]

Lyall, I. T. (1972) The polar low over Britain. Weather, 27, pp. 378-390.

Lyall, I. T. (1972) Summer and sunspots. Weather, 27, pp. 434. [LETTER]

Lyall, I. T. (1972) Thundery outbreaks over southern England with surface south- easterly winds. Weather, 27, pp. 43. [LETTER]

Lyall, I. T. (1973) A heavy rainfall in the East Midlands. Weather, 28, pp. 289- 293.

Lyall, I. T. (1973) Low temperatures in southern Britain. Weather, 28, pp. 134- 140. [FROST]

Lyall, I. T. (1973) Wanted, a wet summer. Weather, 28, pp. 309. [LETTER]

Lyall, I. T. (1974) Next winter? Weather, 29, pp. 390-391. [LETTER, SEASONAL PREDICTION]

Lyall, I. T. (1974) Prediction of warm days in July and August. Weather, 29, pp. 77-78. [LETTER]

Lyall, I. T. (1974) The Shetland thunderstorm of 16 August 1973. Weather, 29, pp. 392. [LETTER, SCOTLAND]

Lyall, I. T. (1974) Some synoptic aspects of hot weather in Britain. Weather, 29, pp. 358-368.

Lyall, I. T. (1974) Weather on Mars. Weather, 29, pp. 28-33. [PLANETARY ATMOSPHERES]

Lyall, I. T. (1974) Weather on Mars. Weather, 29, pp. 356. [LETTER, PLANETARY ATMOSPHERES]

Lyall, I. T. (1975) Cumulus clouds induced by gas. Weather, 30, pp. 342-343. [FUMULUS, LETTER]

Lyall, I. T. (1975) Some synoptic aspects of hot weather in Britain. Weather, 30, pp. 343. [LETTER]

Lyall, I. T. (1975) The winter of 1974-75. Weather, 30, pp. 306-307. [LETTER]

Lyall, I. T. (1976) Indian Monsoons and European anticyclones. Weather, 31, pp. 197. [INDIA, READERS' FORUM]

Lyall, I. T. (1976) Recent trends in British October weather. Weather, 31, pp. 322-327.

Lyall, I. T. (1976) Weather of the 1970s. Weather, 31, pp. 29-30. [LETTER]

Lyall, I. T. (1977) Kew temperatures and the Poulter index. Weather, 32, pp. 313. [LETTER, SUMMER INDEX]

Lyall, I. T. (1977) The London heat-island in June-July 1976. Weather, 32, pp. 296-302.

Lyall, I. T. (1977) One-day discussion meeting short-period weather forecasting. Weather, 32, pp. 151-153. [MEETING REPORT]

Lyall, I. T. (1977) Some local temperature variations in North-east Derbyshire. Weather, 32, pp. 141-145.

Lyall, I. T. (1977) Weather at Kew, August 1973-July 1976. Weather, 32, pp. 187- 189.

Lyall, I. T. (1978) Anomalous weather patterns and long-range forecasting. Weather, 33, pp. 158-159. [LETTER]

Lyall, I. T. (1979) Autumn 1978. Weather, 34, pp. 206. [LETTER]

Lyall, I. T. (1979) Early warm spells - a case study: 2 March 1977. Weather, 34, pp. 10-15.

Lyall, I. T. (1979) Local climates. Weather, 34, pp. 117-119. [MEETING REPORT]

Lyall, I. T. (1980) The growth of barley and the effect of climate. Weather, 35, pp. 271-276. [AGRICULTURAL METEOROLOGY]

Lyall, I. T. (1981) A cylindrical cross-section analysis of the rainstorm of 8-9 September 1972. Weather, 36, pp. 263-266.

Lyall, I. T. (1981) Jamaica's hurricane season: a possible teleconnection? Weather, 36, pp. 89. [LETTER]

Lyall, I. T. (1981) Monthly temperature ranges. Weather, 36, pp. 188-189. [LETTER]

Lyall, I. T. (1982) Preliminary investigation of a Nottinghamshire frost-hollow. Weather, 37, pp. 184-186.

Lyall, I. T. (1982) Weather in April 1981. Weather, 37, pp. 248-249. [LETTER, SNOW]

www.ingramcontent.com/pod-product-compliance
Lightning Source LLC
Chambersburg PA
CBHW041221270326
41932CB00003B/15